ISO/IEC 27001:2022

An introduction to information security and
the ISMS standard

T0046397

ISO/IEC 27001:2022

An introduction to information security
and the ISMS standard

STEVE G WATKINS

IT Governance Publishing

Every possible effort has been made to ensure that the information contained in this book is accurate at the time of going to press, and the publisher and the author cannot accept responsibility for any errors or omissions, however caused. Any opinions expressed in this book are those of the author, not the publisher. Websites identified are for reference only, not endorsement, and any website visits are at the reader's own risk. No responsibility for loss or damage occasioned to any person acting, or refraining from action, as a result of the material in this publication can be accepted by the publisher or the author.

IT Governance Publishing Ltd
Unit 3, Clive Court
Bartholomew's Walk
Cambridgeshire Business Park
Ely, Cambridgeshire
CB7 4EA
United Kingdom
www.itgovernancepublishing.co.uk

Formerly published as *An Introduction to Information Security and ISO27001:2013 – A Pocket Guide* by IT Governance Publishing in 2013.

This edition first published in the United Kingdom in 2022 by IT Governance Publishing.

ISBN 978-1-78778-403-1

ABOUT THE AUTHOR

Steve G Watkins:

Steve is a Director of Kinsnall Consulting Ltd, providing board-level advice on cyber security and related standards.

Steve is an active member of SC 27, the international committee responsible for cyber security, information security and privacy protection standards, including the ISO 27001 family. He Chairs the UK national committee (IST 33) that mirrors SC 27 and is the Chair of the UK ISO/IEC 27001 User Group.

He is also a contracted ISMS and ITSMS Technical Assessor for UKAS, supporting the assessment of certification bodies offering accredited certification to ISO/IEC 27001 and ISO/IEC 20000-1.

Steve managed the world's first successful BS 7799 (the forerunner of ISO 27001) implementation project and is co-author (with Alan Calder) of the definitive compliance guide, *IT Governance – An International Guide to Data Security and ISO 27001/ISO 27002.*[1]

He ran the professional services division of an AIM-listed company that included supporting in excess of 850 ISO 27001 certification projects, supporting clients varying from a 1-person business through to some listed on the FTSE 100.

Contact:

Steve can be contacted through:

www.kinsnall.com

---

[1] For more information, visit:
www.itgovernance.co.uk/shop/product/it-governance-an-international-guide-to-data-security-and-iso27001iso27002-7th-edition.

CONTENTS

INTRODUCTION

This pocket guide is intended to meet the needs of two groups:

1. Individual readers who have turned to it as an introduction to a topic that they know little about.
2. Organisations implementing, or considering implementing, some sort of information security management regime, particularly if using ISO/IEC 27001:2022, that wish to raise awareness.

In either case the guide gives readers an understanding of the basics of information security, including:

- A definition of information security;
- How managing information security can be achieved using an approach recognised worldwide as good practice;
- The factors that need to be considered in an information security regime, including how the perimeters of such a scheme can be properly defined;
- How an information security management system (ISMS) can ensure it is maximising the effect of any budget it has;
- Key areas of investment for a business-focused ISMS; and
- How organisations can demonstrate the degree of assurance they offer with regard to information security, how to interpret claims of adherence to the ISO 27001 standard and exactly what that means.

Corporate bodies will find this guide useful at a number of stages in any information security project, including:

- At the decision-making stage, to ensure that those committing to an information security project do so from a suitably informed position;

- At project initiation, as an introduction to information security for the project board, project team members and other key contributors; and
- As part of an ongoing awareness campaign, being made available to all staff[2] and to new starters as part of their induction.

Corporate users may find they get the most benefit by making this pocket guide available and adding a small flyer inside it, which explains how various sections relate to their own specific environment, or where the issues raised in this guide are addressed in their own ISMS. For example:

**A Real
Co Ltd**

When things go wrong: (Chapter 5)

When you witness a security event you are required to report it in accordance with DOC 16.1, Reporting Information Security Events procedure.

This pocket guide is designed to be read without having to break frequently from the text, but there is a list of abbreviations along with terms and definitions in *Chapter 7* for easy reference.

---

[2] Conducting surveys of people's understanding of information security and compiling the results before and after the start of an awareness campaign enables you to demonstrate the effectiveness of your communications. The results can feed into your management review; see ISO 27001:2022 sections 7.2, 9.1.a and 9.3.c.2.

Where footnotes have been added they are not essential reading, and it is recommended you ignore these on your first read through if you are new to the subject – on a second reading they will be of more relevance, and particularly if you are involved in an information security project or decision.

A word of warning: this is not an implementation or 'How-to' guide.

Implementing an ISO 27001-compliant ISMS requires more advice than a pocket guide such as this could possibly offer. The project is in most cases likely to equate to a significant business-change project and will require all the project governance arrangements that suit such an undertaking.

There are books available that offer suitably detailed advice, such as *IT Governance – A Manager's Guide to Data Security and ISO 27001/ISO 27002.* They can be obtained along with numerous other helpful advice, tools and related information from the sources signposted in *Chapter 7*.

CHAPTER 1: INFORMATION SECURITY – WHAT'S THAT?

To understand what information security means, let's consider something that we all understand the value of: money.

Considering the various aspects of how you look after and use your money, the following emerge as valuable and noteworthy:

Aspect one

> *You do not want other people spending your money, or at least anyone not given your permission to spend it. This means limiting access to your money, or, when considering information instead of money, keeping it **confidential**.*

This makes good sense, and at first pass may seem to be the only thing that matters. However, if restricting access to your money is all that matters, you could store it in a totally sealed iron box. Not very useful when you want to spend it yourself! This brings us on to our second aspect:

Aspect two

> *You want to be able to spend your money when you want to. This means you value its availability. You also need it to be **available** in a usable format and timely manner, so if you are abroad you want the money to be in the correct currency when you come to spend it.*

This also makes good sense. We have identified that in controlling our money we need to consider both restricting access to it (an appropriate degree of confidentiality as far as information is concerned) and ensuring this is balanced with a suitable degree of availability – this applies to information as well. There is another value that we should be concerned with, and to explain this we might consider the process of spending a little further.

Aspect three

> *When making an electronic payment for a purchase, you rely on the figures presented on-screen as reflecting the total cost of the transaction. You would rightly feel aggrieved if the amount that was debited from your account was considerably higher. This demonstrates the value of the cost shown on-screen being accurate and showing all the relevant fees (for a ticket reseller, say): the figure should be complete and accurate.*

There are a number of examples that easily demonstrate the value of information being complete and accurate given how that information is used to inform decisions. Whether it be the information available to potential investors for a stock market float, the medical information for a patient undergoing an operation, or the speedometer in your car, the completeness and accuracy of the information is important. ***Integrity*** is used to describe the 'complete and accurate' attribute of information.

So with money, we value keeping it out of the hands of others, having it accessible when we want it and that numbers representing money are accurate.

When referring to information, this is the equivalent of valuing the information's:

1. **Confidentiality**;
2. **Availability**; and
3. **Integrity**.

Hence, when managing the security of information, we need to consider these three aspects – much more than the layman's understanding of the word 'security'!

Organisations that wish to manage their information security stance typically rely on policies, procedures, guidelines, and associated resources and activities to ensure they are appropriately safeguarding the ***confidentiality***, ***integrity*** and ***availability*** (the more usual order of detailing the three attributes is C, then I and then A), of their information. These arrangements are usually described as an ISMS.

Who does it matter to?

Given the definition of information security as the preservation of the CIA of information,[3] it is relatively easy to determine why this might be of importance to individuals companies and other organisations.

It soon becomes obvious that it is not just the information that we need to be concerned with, but the arrangements for storing, handling, moving and processing it; they all have an effect on the preservation of CIA of the information. Subsequently, to safeguard information security we need to consider the systems we use to store and process it on.

Individuals (members of the public or customers and staff) will want to know that information held about them is being managed and protected appropriately. Theft or fraud involving payment cards, credit ratings and people's identities are well-publicised issues that mean information security is worthy of attention.

Organisations will be driven by at least two factors: the requirements of their stakeholders and/or customers to protect the information they entrust to them, and the need to remain competitive, protecting their intellectual property rights, reputation and list of customers in many instances. Public-sector organisations have similar drivers to maintain a strong security stance and safeguard against security incidents.

---

[3] ISO/IEC 27000:2018 defines information security as the *"preservation of confidentiality, integrity and availability of information"*.
It then has a note that reads; *"In addition, other properties such as authenticity, accountability, non-repudiation and reliability can also be involved"*.

In fact, many sectors are subject to regulations that demand a suitable extent of information management be in place for anyone operating in that sector.

Reliance on suppliers for key services and processes heightens the need for information security assurance through the supply chain. Contracts regularly require an information governance regime in one guise or another.[4]

The other key driver is the need to maintain a competitive edge. The obvious aims of not informing competitors of your costs, customers or trade secrets are concerns that fall within the remit of information security management, as are the less obvious benefits of effective information security such as improvements in customer service through appropriately managed databases (e.g. no longer sending mail shots to addresses that the client has told you it has moved from).

An effective information security management regime can provide an organisation with the foundations on which to build a knowledge management strategy and realise the true value of all the information that it holds.

The public sector has its own drivers, of course, including issues such as justice and national security. There is also the responsibility to be as effective and efficient as possible in conducting work to be able to truly demonstrate appropriate stewardship of public funds.

In addition, staff will expect their personal information to be managed appropriately and their right to privacy respected.

---

[4] More on what assurances such schemes provide and how to interpret claims of conformity is provided in *Chapter 6*.

CHAPTER 2: IT'S NOT IT

The key message in this chapter is that an effective ISMS needs to address issues relating to personnel, facilities, suppliers and cultural issues, in addition to the obvious area of information technology. Information security is a topic that goes well beyond the remit of IT, whether that be the equipment, department or service.[5]

An international standard that defines information security controls for managing information and cyber security risks, ISO 27002:2022, brigades them under the headings: organizational, people, physical and technological, with 59 of the 93 controls detailed being outside of technological.

Having identified what information security is, and recognising it as something worthy of attention, the next stage is to determine exactly what areas and aspects of the organisation will be affected.

Starting with the source of the challenge, we need to consider the 'external and internal issues' that are likely to affect our business, 'interested parties' (e.g. regulators, stakeholders and clients) and the information security requirements of these parties to ensure that the ISMS is relevant to our organisation and provides an appropriate assurance to our stakeholders. It is then a case of considering everything that can affect our information, which means including all the equipment on which that information is held, how it is moved/transmitted and any

---

[5] Cyber security, a discipline closely related to information security, is concerned with the protection of people, society, organisations and nations from cyber risks, whereas information security focuses on the management of the confidentiality, integrity and availability of information.

aspects of the business that can affect the information, equipment and related processes.

There will be aspects that are not directly within management control – this means that it is necessary to consider the dependencies and interfaces of our management system and the information it safeguards with those external factors. The limit of what we can manage is described in a scope statement that considers both physical and logical perimeters. For example, if we consider information that is stored in the Cloud, where the Cloud environment is provided by a third party, then the security requirements placed on the Cloud provider through a contractual agreement are of concern – we need to be clear on the extent to which this is directly managed by those running the ISMS or that those within the ISMS manage the hosting provider to ensure it applies the appropriate security measures.

With regard to confidentiality, it is necessary to consider everyone who has access to the information, the equipment on which it is stored and the systems used to access it. This is likely to include systems maintenance staff and cleaners, in addition to directly employed staff.

The ISMS also needs to address the management of information in different formats, including electronic form and hard copy documents. With information in transit – whether it be in the form of papers being taken home for reviewing the night before a meeting, or records being sent to archive – it becomes obvious that hard copy documents warrant a similar degree of protection to electronic copies. If a trade secret is accessed by a competitor, it does not matter whether it is in an email attachment or printed on a piece of paper: the information that was meant to be kept confidential is in the hands of someone it was not intended to be, or is available via a means that results in unauthorised access and so any value attached to maintaining its confidentiality is compromised. The value of information is often in its content and not solely in the format it is stored or available in.

Considering these issues, one way or another the ISMS needs to define how it addresses relationships with suppliers, business partners, customers and staff. Of course, the facilities and equipment used to protect and provide information are of equal importance, and must also be considered within the scope of the ISMS.

In defining the remit of the ISMS this way, the organisation is stating the business activities over which the ISMS provides assurance. Given the personnel, facilities, suppliers and cultural issues that need to be considered and addressed within the system, it is obviously a topic that goes well beyond the remit of the IT department.

CHAPTER 3: ISO 27001 AND THE MANAGEMENT SYSTEM REQUIREMENTS

As with most topics, there are international standards that deal with information security management, and the main one is ISO 27001:2022.[6]

The Standard is structured in a linear fashion, from the establishment of the ISMS through to its review and adaptation. However, addressing the requirements in that order is not a requirement. In earlier editions, the Standard aligned to the well-recognised Plan-Do-Check-Act (PDCA) model of continual improvement, suggesting this was the best means of designing, developing and implementing an effective ISMS. While this is no longer strictly mandated by ISO 27001, it remains one valid and effective approach.

The PDCA cycle can be summarised as:

- **Plan** what you need to do to achieve the objective (which includes defining what that objective is);
- **Do** what you planned;
- **Check** that what you have done achieves what you had planned for it to achieve and identify any gaps or shortfalls (i.e. check whether you have met the objectives); and
- **Act** on the findings of the check phase to address the gaps and/or improve the efficiency and effectiveness of what you have in place.

---

[6] Previous standards that have set requirements for information security management include BS 7799 and ISO 17799, but ISO 27001 is now the Standard for the specification of an ISMS. ISO 27002 details a set of information security controls and guidance related to them – the same controls are listed in Annex A of ISO 27001.

Typically, this last stage will involve making a plan to further refine and enhance the ISMS, doing what that plan entails, checking that the objectives were achieved, identifying any shortfalls and then acting on the findings by once again creating a plan.

And so, with the introduction of an ISMS using PDCA, the initial cycle of continual improvement is effected, and in practice other PDCA cycles are instigated that progress to different timelines in parallel.

One common misunderstanding in adopting the PDCA approach is that the planning stage is limited purely to planning the project. However, applying the approach required in the first (2005) version of ISO 27001, the planning stage includes all the activity to determine what is required of the ISMS, and how this is to be achieved. This is a significant undertaking, to the extent that it can take up to half of the project time from initiation through to having a full ISMS in place. The other main resource-demanding stage is implementation. The next chapter deals with the most resource-intensive aspects of determining what is required of the ISMS.

There are a number of requirements for a management system to operate that are as applicable to an ISMS as to any other management system. These include:

- **Documented information:** This clause requires the organisation to manage the availability of documents within the ISMS, ensuring the current approved version is available where it is needed. The documents this applies to typically include:
  o The corporate-level policies;
  o Operating procedures that describe the processes that support the policy and explain who does what, where and when;
  o Work instructions that detail how certain tasks should be conducted;

o Records that capture the information that is essential for the purposes of review and to inform decisions. These include documents such as audit schedules and logs, records of work completed for the purpose of traceability and accountability, etc.; and

o Documents sourced from outside of the organisation.

The aim of document control is to ensure that all these documents have been written and approved by the right people and that only the latest approved versions are available to those who need to be aware of and follow them. Records must also be safeguarded once they are generated. This means protecting the CIA of them to be sure they can be retrieved by the right (authorised) people when needed, that they are legible and have not been interfered with.

Returning to the common management system 'hygiene' factors...

- **Internal audit**

  Internal audits can be used for many purposes, but one of the main objectives of deploying an internal management system audit programme is to monitor compliance between the management system requirements and working practice. The internal audits are commissioned by the organisation, for the organisation, and provide an opportunity to review the level of compliance within, and effectiveness of, the ISMS. This is achieved by examining what actually happens across a sample of activities and processes and comparing this to what the management system describes. The identification of any mismatch during an audit provides the opportunity to put it right, either by changing the system description of what happens, where possible by enhancing working practices, or addressing competency issues (often through further training and awareness). The internal audit process should also inform the continual improvement of the ISMS. However, this typically only starts to become an objective of audits once the ISMS is embedded. Internal audits can also be commissioned to target specific areas of concern or to identify opportunities for improvement.

- **Management review**

  Given that management initiates the ISMS by approving the use of resources to undertake the project and issuing the corporate information security policy defining the objectives of the ISMS, it is reasonable to expect them to review the progress of the implementation project and the effectiveness of the ISMS thereafter. The management review is typically held once every 6 or 12 months and is intended to achieve exactly these objectives. A number of reports would be prepared for consideration, covering key indicators of how the ISMS is operating. These reports include an analysis of the outcome of audits (internal, second- and third-party[7]), significant security-related incidents, changes in external and internal issues that may affect the ISMS, an indicator of awareness of information security issues and the ISMS across all those external and internal issues that may affect the ISMS and information security performance. The review should also examine the effectiveness measures[8] that have been developed and

---

[7] See *Chapter 6* for further information on second- and third-party audits.

[8] ISO 27001:2022 requires the organisation to define how the effectiveness of the ISMS will be measured (including in sections 5.1 d, 6.1.1.e.2, 7.2 c, 9.1 and, in particular, 9.1.b) and for management to consider them (section 9.3.c.2).

the nature and timeliness of continual improvement activity that has been identified and/or implemented.

The arrangements for document control and continual improvement can usefully be introduced at the outset of an ISMS project, providing arrangements to support the project and to ensure familiarity with any changes to working practices that need to continue once the initial project has delivered and as the ISMS becomes part of business as usual.

CHAPTER 4: LEGAL, REGULATORY AND CONTRACTUAL REQUIREMENTS AND BUSINESS RISK

The particular security profile an ISMS provides for an organisation is aligned to its business activities and objectives. The organisation identifies its interested parties – from stakeholders to staff to customers and the public – and their requirements for information security. These requirements, together with the organisation's specific legal, regulatory and contractual obligations, form the starting point of the ISMS security arrangements, and these are combined with the results of an information security risk assessment to determine the blend of security controls on which the organisation will rely.

ISO 27001 does not dictate a particular methodology for the information security risk assessment and there are many to choose from. What follows here is a general description of an information security risk assessment you might expect to see in an effective ISMS.

To undertake the information security risk assessment, it is necessary to have defined the scope of the ISMS. This is achieved by identifying the relevant issues and requirements of interested parties and the business activities that the ISMS is to encompass. The boundary of the ISMS can then be determined, along with the interfaces and dependences of the ISMS with activities undertaken by others outside of the scoped organisation.

For the risk assessment to be effective, the organisation must consider everything that might go wrong with respect to the information the ISMS is intended to safeguard – this will need to include information, information processing and storage equipment (every server, computer, laptop, mobile phone and

Cloud services), systems, staff, buildings, etc.[9] The reliance on suppliers and others that can affect the CIA of the information will also need to be considered.

Risks need to be identified and estimated for CIA in a manner whereby the results of the assessment are comparable and reproducible. The 'consequence' assigned to each risk reflects the total cost to the organisation if that risk were to materialise, from the cost of replacement, to the consequences for the process(es) it is involved in, to the impact on the organisation's reputation. This is normally best estimated by those involved in the relevant business processes.

These consequence values provide the impact aspect of the classic

Risk[10] = Likelihood × Impact

relationship.

The risk assessment then uses these estimates, and those of the likelihood of the risk coming to fruition, to determine the risk values. The relationship between likelihood, impact and risk is demonstrated in the following diagram, in this case showing three levels of likelihood and three levels of impact, which

---

[9] Advice on information security risk assessments is more complex than can be covered in this pocket guide. See Information Security Risk Management for ISO 27001/ISO 27002 by Alan Calder and Steve G Watkins:

www.itgovernancepublishing.co.uk/product/information-security-risk-management-for-iso-27001-iso-27002-third-edition.

[10] ISO 27000:2018 defines risk as the *"effect of uncertainty on objectives"* and goes on to state in a note that *"information security risk is associated with the potential that threats will exploit vulnerabilities of an information asset of group of information assets and thereby cause harm to an organization"*.

together give five levels of risk varying from 'very low' to 'very high':

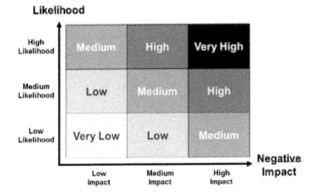

Figure 1: Risk assessment

The main aim of an ISMS is to manage all risks to a consistent level, and management needs to determine what level of risk is acceptable. For example, management may, using the diagram above, decide that risks up to and including 'low'[11] are acceptable, and that therefore it is only those risks that have been assessed as falling above that level of 'risk acceptance criteria' that need managing. In terms of the diagram, the risk acceptance level can be demonstrated by the shaded area as shown here:

---

[11] Defining the graduations on the impact and likelihood scales informs what a 'low risk' equates to, and helps ensure that the assessed risks are comparable and reproducible.

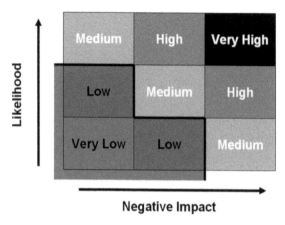

Figure 2: Risk assessment criteria

Each organisation will have a different level of risk acceptance and this will relate to the organisation's risk appetite – the degree of risk that it is happy to live with on a day-to-day basis. Each risk is assigned to a risk owner, who will be responsible for approving the risk treatment and accepting any residual risk, in light of the risk acceptance criteria.

Risks assessed as falling above the acceptable level are considered and a decision taken as to what to do about each of them. This decision determines which one or more of the following options to apply to address the identified risk:

1. Apply controls to reduce the risk. (Treat)
2. Accept the risk; this is normally determined by the risk acceptance criteria, but can occasionally be applied even if the risk level is above the acceptable level. (Tolerate)
3. Avoid the risk by identifying a workaround that negates the risk. (Terminate)
4. Transfer the business risk to an insurer or supplier. (Transfer)

As different decisions and controls are selected for application to various risks, the risk assessment is re-estimated and this process continues until all the assessed risks are estimated to meet the risk acceptance criteria.

The process of determining controls to manage risk is critical to the performance of the ISMS. In the first stage, you should design a set of controls to manage the risk, followed by comparing this list of controls to those in Annex A of ISO 27001. Information security controls can and should be taken from any valid source appropriate to the organisation or process, including designing them yourself – it is the process of comparing them against the candidate controls in Annex A that ensures none have been inappropriately omitted.

To deliver the appropriate countermeasures against information security risks, the ISMS needs to ensure that the controls identified as necessary through the risk assessment process (these typically include those required by legal, regulatory and contractual obligations) are in place and applied effectively. Appropriate measures are also required for processes, products and services provided from beyond the scope of the ISMS – whether from another part of the same entity/group or an external supplier – to support the ISMS and ensure information security. By informing the selection of information security controls with this approach, an organisation can ensure that it is maximising the effectiveness of its information security spend, and not leaving one area of risk open to exploitation at the cost of an inconsistently high level of control elsewhere.

ISO 27001 requires a document to be produced that details which controls are applied within the ISMS and which are not. This is known as the 'Statement of Applicability' (SoA) – it states which controls are, or are not, applied within the ISMS.

The process to determine the right blend of security controls within the ISMS requires a degree of central coordination and often benefits from the use of a suitable software solution that can automate many of the potentially resource-intensive administration aspects of the process. The return on investing in information security risk assessment software includes the efficiencies it offers when revisiting the risk assessment, as required by the standard on a periodic basis or when changes occur. Having software that maintains audit trails of changes and updates to risk estimates helps hugely and addresses one of the tasks necessary even as the ISMS becomes part of business-as-usual (BAU).

CHAPTER 5: INFORMATION SECURITY CONTROLS

Having gained an appreciation of the methodical approach to the selection of information security controls and other ways of addressing risks, it is time to examine the security controls defined in the international ISMS standards.

The standards emphasise that the controls they detail are to be used to ensure that none have been inappropriately omitted and that they are not a default control set to select from. Typically, an organisation would start with sector- and contract-specific requirements and then consider others. There will also be technological developments that introduce risks which are not covered to a suitable extent by the security controls listed in Annex A of ISO 27001, and so it may be necessary to adopt further controls.

In ISO 27001 there are 93 controls split across 4 themes:

1. Organizational controls;
2. People controls;
3. Physical controls; and
4. Technological controls.

As well as providing a means of brigading the controls, these four themes emphasise that effective information security requires much more than a technological solution – the 'organizational controls' category has the most individual controls listed (37), although it is closely followed by 'technological controls' (34).

The four themes can be summarised as:

1. **'People'** – contains controls that relate to individual people;

2. **'Physical'** – contains controls that relate to physical objects and services that affect them (e.g. utilities and equipment maintenance);
3. **'Technological'** – deals with technology; and
4. **'Organizational'** – accommodates everything else, including those people-related controls that go beyond the individual.

Each of the controls in ISO 27001:2022 Annex A is described in further detail in ISO 27002:2022, where they have five attributes defined along with a purpose, guidance and other information. The five attributes enable the controls to be filtered for the purpose of risk treatment. The attributes, with the possibilities for each, are:

- **Control type:** Preventive, Detective, Corrective. (*The combination and balance of control types is important for effective risk mitigation.*)
- **Information security properties:** Confidentiality, Integrity and Availability.
- **Cybersecurity concepts:** Identify, Protect, Detect, Respond and Recover.
  (*These reflect the concepts in ISO/IEC TS 27110, a standard on cyber security frameworks, and the NIST standards.*)
- **Operational capabilities, (*a view on the controls from a practitioner's perspective*):** Governance, Asset management, Information protection, Human resource security, Physical security, System and network security, Application security, Secure configuration, Identity and access management, Threat and vulnerability management, Continuity, Supplier relationships security, Legal and compliance, Information security event management, and Information security assurance.

- **Security domains:** Governance and ecosystem, Protection, Defence and resilience. *(Aligned with the ENISA security measures for operators of essential services.[12])*

Returning to the ISO/IEC 27001:2022 Annex A controls split across those four themes:

1. Organizational controls

This theme can be considered as accommodating many of the controls off which the rest of the system hangs. There is a need for a corporate-level information security policy, which is a statement of the organisation's commitment and objectives relating to information security, and other policies that support and deliver the intent of this. The highest-level policy needs to be available to everyone required to abide by it, which could include suppliers, business partners, customers and staff.

There is a need to define where responsibilities for information security lie within the organisation, and through appropriate segregation of duties make sure that this avoids opportunities for abuse. A similar set of requirements are implied in the control for project management and those for supplier relationships – ensuring respective roles, responsibilities, actions and liabilities for information security are agreed and documented. There are further controls dedicated to supplier management, ensuring resilience in the supply chain, and one specifically for the use of Cloud-based services.

---

[12] See CG Publication 01/2018 – Reference document on security measures for Operators of Essential Services:

- *http://ec.europa.eu/newsroom/dae/document.cfm?doc_id=5364 3*; and
- *https://www.enisa.europa.eu/topics/nis-directive/minimum-security-measures-for-operators-of-essentials-services*.

The topic of asset management has five controls that go from having an asset inventory, to defining acceptable use, to classification and labelling schemes and information transfer. An information classification scheme will set out how different levels of sensitive information (whether it is sensitive due to its confidential nature, or one of the other attributes) are to be handled and that this is clearly indicated through a labelling convention. Access control is covered here, including ensuring that the right people have access to the right things and that those people use appropriate means of demonstrating they are who they are. Access management relates to both logical and/or physical barriers.

Passwords and user IT accounts are typical logical access controls and are of course only as robust as the practices that manage them. Eradicating poor practices such as writing passwords down, or using sequential or easily guessable combinations, should be avoided, and two-factor or multifactor authentication encouraged – this is covered under 'technological controls' below.

There are a number of controls that deal with the handling of problems, information security events and/or information security incidents. These are additional to the improvement-process requirements of maintaining an ISMS, and cover what should be done in reaction to, and to recover from, a security breach.

The severity of information security breaches can vary massively. If the problem is likely to cause a significant challenge to the normal running of operations, some form of business continuity should be invoked and in doing so information security should not be compromised. This area of control includes the need to regularly test the plans to learn from the experience and improve them before they are called upon for real.

Of course, not all security incidents require such a dramatic response, but the degree of reaction and the method for determining escalation should be defined.

The organizational controls theme addresses legal and compliance issues, with six controls setting out the need to abide by the law and internal requirements, as well as the benefit of checking these arrangements. The controls address respecting others' rights, (particularly with regard to intellectual property rights) as well as protecting the organisation itself. The final control deals with documented procedures as a means of ensuring that there is a common understanding of the what, who, when and how with regard to information security activities.

2. People controls

Managing the human aspect of information security is hugely important – 'squidgy-ware' (the grey matter between people's ears) often lets the side down before the hardware or software associated with IT security – and as such has its own theme. The eight controls here consider the sourcing, vetting, management (people changing roles and disciplinary processes need to consider information security, alongside the more normal day-to-day operations), exiting arrangements and associated documentation for staff, contractors and any other people who interact with the organisation, including anyone who has physical access to any premises at or from which information and related assets can be accessed.

Ensuring individuals are aware of the expectations the organisation has of them, and the consequences of not abiding by them should be part of an information security awareness campaign, including making sure everyone knows how and when to report a possible security breach. The benefit of being informed of a possible breach as soon as possible means all relevant parties, including suppliers, business partners, customers and staff, should be aware of the need and means to report suspected breaches. Cleaners may be among the first people at a site each day, or the last to leave it, and they should be trained and required by contract to report any security-related observations to an appropriate contact.

3. Physical controls

Physical access is, of course, a concern for information security. Anyone who has access to the equipment or media on which information is stored could potentially walk or run away with it and the information stored on it. While some protection can be offered to prevent access to information stolen in this manner (or at least rendering it in an unusable format), it will still affect the availability of that information and possibly the resulting integrity of the data as well.

Perimeters around secure areas should be defined in all three dimensions – tunnelling in through the floor, or using an air vent in the ceiling, may still allow enough access and egress for theft to take place.

The securing of premises and monitoring of physical security are considered, as well as the expectations for those working in secure areas – Can food and drink be consumed? What, if any, recording devices (mobile phones being one of the more obvious) are permitted? Are people allowed to work unsupervised in secure areas?

Storage media, from sourcing it, to use and re-use, to decommissioning/disposal (as with all equipment), requires attention and often dovetails with the classification labelling and handling controls contained in the organizational controls theme described earlier.

There are also controls relating to the dependency on utilities and the environment – power cuts and adverse weather conditions provide regular tests of security arrangements and their ability to make sure the systems and information on which the business relies continue to be available and protected. Cables relating to both utility supplies and those carrying data need protection and equipment needs to be maintained.

4. Technological controls

The 34 technological controls cover issues relating to the broad topics of:

- System, network and endpoint equipment protection;
- Access issues, which dovetail with the 'access control' entry under 'Organizational controls';
- Information management;
- Continuity, focusing on resilience as opposed to safeguarding information security in a business continuity plan invocation scenario that is covered in two controls in 'organizational controls': one titled 'information security during disruptions' and the other 'ICT readiness for business continuity'; and
- Breach management.

Expanding on these in turn:

The controls relating to the protection of systems, networks and endpoints start with addressing the risks of storing, processing and accessing information through user equipment including user-owned devices (bring your own device). The guidance in ISO/IEC 27002:2022 sets out issues to be considered and addressed, including making sure that the user is aware of their responsibilities, and having appropriate technological measures in place. As with many of the controls in Annex A, the means of addressing this particular control relies on arrangements for other controls, in this case including those for data classification (as does information access restrictions – another of the Annex A Technological controls), security of assets off-premises, user monitoring, backups, antivirus and the ability to store information locally.

There are approximately ten controls that focus on the security of the network and systems, ensuring that the deployment and maintenance of them are appropriate. This includes safeguarding against malware and deploying web filtering, patching vulnerabilities, controlling the configurations and software in use, ensuring redundancy of processing capabilities, limiting the use of programs that have enhanced capabilities, and practising good network security.

A variety of tests and monitoring practices can confirm that only the right, approved equipment is connected to the network, that systems and software are as required (including the approved mix of solutions and the number for the licences held), and can include penetration testing to confirm the resilience of the technical measures in place.

A control on cryptography flags the relationship with the organisation's classification scheme and the organisational control for legal compliance given the variety of encryption regulations around the world.

The creation, rollout, maintenance and decommissioning of secure software and systems, as well as architecture and services, are addressed across approximately seven controls that include the need to be clear on security requirements at the outset, testing against those requirements at various stages of development and pre-rollout, having separate environments for development, testing and production as well as appropriate change management measures. These controls include secure coding practices and recognise the importance of supplier management where any aspects of development and maintenance are outsourced, working alongside the organisational controls relating to supplier relationships and agreements.

Weak password practices (user authentication being an 'organizational control') lead to a second level of authentication control, that of 'secure authentication', which brings us into the technological controls that focus on access. Secure authentication involves the use of additional verification measures such as multifactor authentication, where there is a combination of 'something you are' (say, a fingerprint or voice-recognition), 'something you have' (a key or token) and 'something you know' (a passphrase or word).

An example is a debit card being used to withdraw cash from an ATM (the magnetic strip or smart chip being the physical key) and your personal identification number (PIN – the logical key). Of course, when using a payment card online, the physical aspect normally disappears if you have sufficient details to hand in another format, and hence the increasing reliance on one-use codes being texted to your mobile phone number or bank-issued card readers being used to authenticate the transaction.

Access to information and systems should be managed appropriately. Some sensitive systems may require session timeouts, requiring the user to re-enter authentication criteria every so often whether they have been active or not. The functioning of software should be safeguarded by restricting access to the tools and code that would facilitate unauthorised changes.

The allocation and management of privileged access rights is included, requiring appropriate authorisation and limiting the use of those super-user profiles to when they are really necessary.

There are a handful of controls that cover practices such as deletion, data masking (to protect sensitive data, including personally identifiable information (PII), leakage prevention and avoiding unwanted consequences of running audits and tests.

Issues such as backup, redundancy and capacity management are mentioned here, which includes testing of the backup so that, as an example, any accidentally deleted file can be restored from a recent backup.

The remaining technological controls can be considered as relating to breach management, covering the logging of system and user activities, monitoring of networks, systems and applications, and ensuring clock synchronisation to enable timelines to be determined during investigations.

CHAPTER 6: CERTIFICATION

As with many other management system standards, there is a scheme that can be used by organisations to demonstrate their conformity with the internationally recognised standard for an ISMS, ISO/IEC 27001.

Organisations wishing to use this scheme to demonstrate the robustness of their information security management arrangements need to subject themselves to an external audit.

If the audit and resulting certificate is part of the internationally recognised 'accredited certification scheme', then interested parties will have a good idea of the degree of confidence they can put in the issued certificate. Accredited certificates are issued by audit bodies that are accredited by their local accreditation body. In the UK, this means that the United Kingdom Accreditation Service (UKAS) accredits the audit/certification body. Certificates issued under UKAS accreditation will bear the UKAS management systems accreditation symbol:

Figure 3: UKAS management systems accreditation symbol

The four-digit number under the UKAS symbol relates to the accreditation schedule that can be viewed on the UKAS website (*www.ukas.com*) and will be used in conjunction with the certification body's logo.

Organisations seeking to demonstrate they conform with the Standard become certified, not accredited.

Accreditation bodies around the world sign up to a memorandum of understanding that results in mutual recognition of each other's schemes – so a certificate issued under accreditation by the ANSI-ASQ National Accreditation Board (ANAB) in the US, the Joint Accreditation System of Australia and New Zealand (JAS-ANZ) or another member of the International Accreditation Forum (IAF)[13] will be the equivalent of one issued under UKAS accreditation – hence a worldwide scheme exists.

The global scheme enables suppliers to demonstrate that they manage information security in accordance with recognised good practice. The confidence this scheme provides means that customers can put some reliance on certification rather than incur the cost of sending their own auditors in to determine the confidence required by their own directors, stakeholders and clients.[14] This can save a lot of time, cost and disruption for both the auditing and audited parties – a benefit that contributes to the uptake of ISO 27001-accredited certification.

However, claims of ISO 27001 certification are often misinterpreted, or used as a guarantee where they should not be.

---

[13] To find out if an accredited certificate is the equivalent of those issued under the scheme described here, determine whether the accreditation body is a member of the IAF (*www.iaf.nu*).

[14] Some customers may also wish to conduct supplier audits, in which case ISO/IEC 27001 certification could provide the framework, terms and definitions as well as a familiarity for that from the outset.

To gain certification, the organisation needs to comply with ISO 27001, which means that it must have a scope defining the extent of its ISMS (or at least the extent of the ISMS that is certified) and an SoA that defines what controls are applied across which aspects of the ISMS.

It is these two documents, together with the accredited certificate, that provide evidence of the level of assurance the organisation's ISMS provides regarding its information security practices. Certification does not provide any guarantee that there will not be a security breach!

ISO 27001 is not a product certification scheme, and to rely on it as such is nonsensical. Accredited certification to ISO 27001 provides a service assurance. Sometimes a client, regulator or other interested party requires greater confidence than accredited certification provides, in which case ISO/IEC 27001 and accredited certification still provides the benefit of a known approach, framework and terminology that can be referenced for planning, conducting and reporting on an audit with bespoke audit objectives than those for accredited certification.

Other audit applications

The existence of a specification for an ISMS lends itself to supplier or second-party audits. This means that buyers can rely on the Standard to provide a recognised and widely available framework against which to conduct supplier audits. These audits can be used to determine the level of information security management their supplier is exercising.

Second-party audits can be used by both the auditing and audited parties along similar lines as first-party audits (see 'Internal audits' in *Chapter 3*) and third-party audits (see 'Certification audits' in this chapter), benefitting both organisations and driving continual improvement through the supply chain. However, second-party audits can prove expensive and are often only used where the degree of risk warrants them. Often the assurance of accredited certification, together with suitably intelligent questioning, is more cost-effective.

CHAPTER 7: SIGNPOSTING

For access to a comprehensive set of all things relating to information security, see:

www.itgovernance.co.uk

For board-level advice on cyber security and related standards, see:

www.kinsnall.com

For general advice that is as applicable to the home as the office, take a look at:

www.ncsc.gov.uk/cyberaware/home

Terms

Most of the following are explanations of terms used in the ISMS standards. Where a formal definition from ISO/IEC 27000:2018 or ISO/IEC 27002:2022 has been provided, it is marked with an * symbol.

- **Accreditation:** the scheme through which an authoritative body formally recognises a person's or organisation's competence to carry out specified tasks. Not to be confused with certification. Third-party audit bodies have their certification scheme accredited and the organisations they audit, subject to a successful outcome, become certified.
- **Asset:** anything that has value to the organisation.* With regard to information security assets, these are typically brigaded into primary and supporting assets as follows:

Primary assets:

- **Information:** databases and data files, other files and copies of plans, system documentation, original user manuals, original training material, operational or other support procedures, continuity plans, other fall-back arrangements, archived information, financial and accounting information.
- **Business processes and activities:** these set your organisation apart from competitors.

Supporting assets:

- **Software:** application software, operating and system software, development tools and utilities, e-learning assets, network tools and utilities.
- **Physical hardware:** computer equipment (including workstations, notebooks, monitors, modems, scanning machines, printers), communications equipment (routers, mobile phones, voice-conferencing units, etc.), mobile media, other technical equipment (power supplies, air-conditioning units), furniture, lighting, other equipment.
- **Network:** groups of assets that act together to provide computing and communications services.
- **Personnel:** staff and others.

- **Availability:** property of being accessible and usable on demand by an authorized entity.*
- **Certification:** the process through which a certification body confirms that a product, process or service conforms to a specific standard or specification. For example, an organisation's ISMS becomes certified to ISO 27001:2022.

- **Certification body:** *see* Third-party certification body.
- **Compliance:** a positive answer to the question 'Is what is taking place in line with the pre-specified requirements?' Hence, non-compliance and compliance monitoring. Compliance is often used in a legal context.
- **Confidentiality:** property that information is not made available or disclosed to unauthorised individuals, entities, or processes.*
- **Conformity:** fulfilment of a requirement. A positive answer to the question 'Is what is taking place in line with the requirements?' Hence, nonconformity and conformity assessment activity. Conformity is often used in a non-legal context.
- **Document control:** a system whereby all documents within the system are managed in a manner to ensure that the currency of the document is always clear. When a controlled document is amended, all controlled copies of it should be simultaneously updated by the new version.
- **Encryption:** the conversion of data into code, using a mathematical algorithm, to prevent it being understood by a third party.
- **Information security event:** identified occurrence of a system, service or network state indicating a possible breach of information security policy or failure of controls, or a previously unknown situation that can be security relevant.* (*See also* Information security incident).
- **Information security incident:** identified single or series of unwanted or unexpected information security events that have a significant probability of compromising business operations and threatening information security.* (*See also* Information security event *and* Asset).

- **Information security management system (ISMS):** part of the overall management arrangements, based on a risk approach, to establish, implement, operate, monitor, review, maintain and improve information security.
- **Information security policy:** the organisation's policy for securing its information.
- **Integrity:** property of accuracy and completeness.*
- **ISMS:** *see* Information security management system.
- **ISO:** acronym, from the Greek *isos* ('equal to'), adopted by the International Organization for Standardization – the world's largest developer of standards. Its membership comprises the national-standards bodies of countries around the world.
- **ISO/IEC 27002:2022:** the international standard for information security controls. It details 93 information security controls, providing implementation guidance and other relevant information.
- **Policy:** intentions and direction of an organisation, as formally expressed by its top management.*
- **Risk:** effect of uncertainty on objectives.*
  The definition in ISO 27000 goes on to say in notes that risk *"is often characterized by reference to potential events and consequences, or a combination of these"* and that *"risk is often expressed as a combination of the consequences of an event and the associated likelihood of that event occurring"*.
- **Risk acceptance:** informed decision to take a particular risk.*
- **Risk analysis:** process to comprehend the nature of risk and to determine the level of risk.*
- **Risk appetite:** an organisation's overall attitude to risk, the balance between risk and return, usually a strategic decision by the organisation's board.

- **Risk assessment:** overall process of risk identification, risk analysis and risk evaluation.*
- **Risk management:** coordinated activities to direct and control an organisation with regard to risk.* This can involve risk assessment, risk treatment, risk acceptance and risk communication.
- **Statement of Applicability (SoA):** documented statement describing the controls that have been identified as required in the organisation's ISMS. The selection of controls is informed by the results and conclusions of the risk assessment and risk treatment processes.
- **Third-party certification body:** independent organisation with the necessary competence and reliability to award certificates following verification of conformance. It is advisable to check the accreditation status of such bodies before appointing them.
- **Threat:** a potential cause of an unwanted incident, which may result in harm to a system or organisation.*
- **United Kingdom Accreditation Service (UKAS):** the sole national accreditation body recognised by the UK government to assess, against internationally agreed standards, organisations that provide certification, testing, inspection and calibration services. See *www.ukas.com*.
- **Vulnerability:** weakness of an asset or control that can be exploited by one or more threats.*

FURTHER READING

IT Governance Publishing (ITGP) is the world's leading publisher for governance and compliance. Our industry-leading pocket guides, books, training resources and toolkits are written by real-world practitioners and thought leaders. They are used globally by audiences of all levels, from students to C-suite executives.

Our high-quality publications cover all IT governance, risk and compliance frameworks and are available in a range of formats. This ensures our customers can access the information they need in the way they need it.

Our other publications about cyber security include:

- *The Cyber Security Handbook – Prepare for, respond to and recover from cyber attacks* by Alan Calder, *www.itgovernancepublishing.co.uk/product/the-cyber-security-handbook-prepare-for-respond-to-and-recover-from-cyber-attacks*
- *The Ransomware Threat Landscape – Prepare for, recognise and survive ransomware attacks* by Alan Calder, *www.itgovernancepublishing.co.uk/product/the-ransomware-threat-landscape*
- *The Art of Cyber Security – A practical guide to winning the war on cyber crime* by Gary Hibberd, *www.itgovernancepublishing.co.uk/product/the-art-of-cyber-security*

For more information on ITGP and branded publishing services, and to view our full list of publications, visit *www.itgovernancepublishing.co.uk*.

To receive regular updates from ITGP, including information on new publications in your area(s) of interest, sign up for our newsletter at
www.itgovernancepublishing.co.uk/topic/newsletter.

Branded publishing

Through our branded publishing service, you can customise ITGP publications with your company's branding.

Find out more at
www.itgovernancepublishing.co.uk/topic/branded-publishing-services.

Related services

ITGP is part of GRC International Group, which offers a comprehensive range of complementary products and services to help organisations meet their objectives.

For a full range of resources on ISO 27001 visit *www.itgovernance.co.uk/iso27001*.

Training services

The IT Governance training programme is built on our extensive practical experience designing and implementing management systems based on ISO standards, best practice and regulations.

Our courses help attendees develop practical skills and comply with contractual and regulatory requirements. They also support career development via recognised qualifications.

Learn more about our training courses in ISO 27001 and view the full course catalogue at *www.itgovernance.co.uk/training*.

Professional services and consultancy

We are a leading global consultancy of IT governance, risk management and compliance solutions. We advise businesses around the world on their most critical issues and present cost-saving and risk-reducing solutions based on international best practice and frameworks.

We offer a wide range of delivery methods to suit all budgets, timescales and preferred project approaches.

Further reading

Find out how our consultancy services can help your organisation at *www.itgovernance.co.uk/consulting*.

Industry news

Want to stay up to date with the latest developments and resources in the IT governance and compliance market? Subscribe to our Weekly Round-up newsletter and we will send you mobile-friendly emails with fresh news and features about your preferred areas of interest, as well as unmissable offers and free resources to help you successfully start your projects. *www.itgovernance.co.uk/weekly-round-up*.